CREED
YOUTH STUDY BOOK

CREED
WHAT CHRISTIANS BELIEVE AND WHY

Creed
978-1-5018-1371-9
978-1-5018-1372-6 *eBook*
978-1-5018-1373-3 *Large Print*

Creed: DVD
978-1-5018-1376-4

Creed: Leader Guide
978-1-5018-1374-0
978-1-5018-1375-7 *eBook*

Creed: Youth Study Book
978-1-5018-1383-2
978-1-5018-1384-9 *eBook*

Creed: Children's Leader Guide
978-1-5018-1370-2

Creed: Leader Kit
978-1-5018-2483-8

For more information, visit www.AdamHamilton.org.

Also by Adam Hamilton

24 Hours That Changed the World

Christianity and World Religions

Christianity's Family Tree

Confronting the Controversies

Enough

Final Words from the Cross

Forgiveness

Half Truths

John

Leading Beyond the Walls

Love to Stay

Making Sense of the Bible

Not a Silent Night

Revival

Seeing Gray in a
    World of Black and White

Selling Swimsuits in the Arctic

Speaking Well

The Call

The Journey

The Way

Unleashing the Word

When Christians Get It Wrong

Why?

ADAM HAMILTON

CREED

WHAT CHRISTIANS BELIEVE AND WHY

Youth Study Book
Mike Poteet

Abingdon Press / Nashville

CREED
WHAT CHRISTIANS BELIEVE AND WHY
YOUTH STUDY BOOK

This book is printed on elemental chlorine-free paper.
ISBN 978-1-5018-1383-2

16 17 18 19 20 21 22 23 24 25—10 9 8 7 6 5 4 3 2 1
MANUFACTURED IN THE UNITED STATES OF AMERICA

CONTENTS

The Apostles' Creed

I believe in God, the Father Almighty,
   creator of heaven and earth.

I believe in Jesus Christ, his only Son, our Lord,
   who was conceived by the Holy Spirit,
   born of the Virgin Mary,
   suffered under Pontius Pilate,
   was crucified, died, and was buried;
   he descended to the dead.
   On the third day he rose again;
   he ascended into heaven,
   is seated at the right hand of the Father,
   and will come again to judge the living and the dead.

I believe in the Holy Spirit,
   the holy catholic* church,
   the communion of saints,
   the forgiveness of sins,
   the resurrection of the body,
   and the life everlasting. Amen.[1]

*universal

INTRODUCTION

The Need for Creeds

"What do Christians have to believe?"

Maybe someone, a non-Christian friend or relative, has asked you that question. Maybe sometimes you've asked that question yourself.

Honestly, the right answer is "Not much!" It's not as though, when he saw them for the last time, the risen Jesus handed his disciples an advanced theology textbook and said, "Here you go; learn this, and you're good!"

At its core, Christian faith is not about *what* we believe but about *in whom* we believe. We believe in—we trust, we obey, we commit ourselves to worshiping and serving—Jesus. All anyone "has to believe" to be a Christian is one short statement that hasn't changed in two thousand years: "Jesus is Lord" (Romans 10:9; 1 Corinthians 12:3).

Still—*what* we believe about Jesus does matter! What does it *mean* to say he is Lord? As we'll see in this study, the word *Lord* was a loaded one in the first-century world. The Roman emperor claimed the title "Lord" for himself. His Jewish subjects reserved the word *Lord* for the God of Israel. What did the earliest Christians mean, calling a crucified rabbi and wonder-worker from Nazareth *Lord*? They needed, and wanted, to give an account of how, in this Jesus, they had encountered God.

Over its first several centuries, the church developed doctrine (official teaching) to clarify what it meant when it referred to Jesus as Lord. Experience came first; doctrine came later. And sometimes the church summarized its doctrine in short, definitive statements of belief called creeds.

The Apostles' Creed

Church legend says Simon Peter and the other apostles wrote the creed that now bears their collective name on the Day of Pentecost, when the Holy Spirit filled the church with power for mission (Acts 2). Each of the twelve men proclaimed a truth he knew to be essential: One said, "I believe in God, the Father almighty"; another, "who made heaven and earth"; and so on.

In truth, the Apostles' Creed as we have it today developed from the Christian baptismal practice as far back as the middle of the second century. Candidates for church membership (called "catechumens," *kat-uh-KYOO-mens*) would spend Lent (the forty days, not counting Sundays, before Easter) in prayer, fasting, and studying Christian belief. When they entered the baptismal waters, the priest would ask them whether they believed in God the Father, God the Son, and God the Spirit; an immersion in the water followed each answer of "*Credo*," Latin for "I believe."[1]

Although not written by the apostles themselves, the Creed is a legitimate summary of apostolic teaching. Does it cover *everything* the apostles taught about Jesus? No—for example, it never makes a direct statement about Jesus' fully divine and fully human nature. But has it proven itself a useful review of major teachings that all Christians hold in common? Absolutely.

As John Dickson, an ordained Anglican minister who teaches at the University of Sydney, has said, "In my tradition...as in the Roman Catholic, and Presbyterian, and tons of other denominations, the Apostles' Creed is a regular part of worship....The beauty of having it in a service is that it clarifies everything, so that no matter what's been preached on, you come back to this. Here's the center of the faith."[2]

About This Resource

This Youth Study Book surveys the content of the Apostles' Creed. It follows the structure of Adam Hamilton's book *Creed: What Christians Believe and Why.* It also covers some of the same Scriptures and ideas in Hamilton's book, but it can be used on its own as well as part of a congregational study program. This resource can be used in small-group settings or by individuals.

Each chapter follows the same format:

- *Pray a Psalm*—Begin your time of study by praying with words from the Psalter. Each psalm selection connects to the theme of the chapter.
- *Get the Conversation Rolling*—"Break the ice" in a group setting or simply stimulate your own thinking by rolling a six-sided die (more than once, if you like) and answering the appropriate question.
- *Consider the Creed*—Each essay offers explanation and discussion of important themes in each chapter's portion of the Creed, followed by questions to prompt individual or group reflection and conversation.
- *Reflect with Scripture*—Read and answer questions about a Bible passage that relates to the themes of the chapter's portion of the Creed. These are not "proof texts" for the Creed, but offer biblical "entry points" into thinking about its content.
- *Suggested Activities*—These options provide additional ways to engage with the Creed.
- *What Do You Believe?*—This section gives participants the chance to make their own statements of faith.

The second chapter, covering the Creed's teaching about Jesus, offers roughly twice as much content in the essay and activities as the others. Readers using this resource in a group setting may choose to cover this content in two sessions, the first focusing on the phrase "Jesus Christ, [God's] only Son, our Lord"; and the other covering the Creed's account of Jesus' life, work, and promised return.

Christians believe we are saved by God's grace alone. We can't work our way into salvation, and we don't earn God's favor through our beliefs. But our beliefs do matter. May using this resource help you discover the rich depths of faith proclaimed in the Apostles' Creed, and may it enhance your faith as you follow Jesus, the Lord.

1.
GOD

I believe in God, the Father Almighty,
creator of heaven and earth.

PRAY A PSALM

Where could I go to get away from your spirit?
　　Where could I go to escape your presence?
If I went up to heaven, you would be there.
　　If I went down to the grave, you would be there too!
If I could fly on the wings of dawn,
　　stopping to rest only on the far side of the ocean—
　　　　even there your hand would guide me;
　　　　even there your strong hand would hold me tight!
If I said, "The darkness will definitely hide me;
　　the light will become night around me,"

> *even then the darkness isn't too dark for you!*
> *Nighttime would shine bright as day,*
> *because darkness is the same as light to you!*
> —*Psalm 139:7-12*

GET THE CONVERSATION ROLLING

Roll a six-sided die and answer the corresponding question from the list below.

1. What sight, sound, or smell do you associate with God, and why?
2. Name one actor and one actress you would cast as God in a movie, and briefly explain your choices.
3. If you were God and wanted to prove your existence to the world, what would you do?
4. What's one thing you wished everyone believed about God?
5. What currently popular, nonreligious song most makes you think about God, and why?
6. If you could ask God to do any one thing to prove God's existence, what would you ask for?

CONSIDER THE CREED

Can We Talk About God Without Blushing?

Early in June 2016, a certain piece of "news" flooded my social media feeds. Theoretical physicist Dr. Michio Kaku had supposedly made a stunning announcement. One website breathlessly declared:

World Renowned Scientist Michio Kaku Proves Existence Of God[1]

Turns out, he didn't.

As I followed a long trail of hyperlinks away from that clickbait headline, I never found a source I could trust telling me when, where, or to whom Dr. Kaku had made this groundbreaking revelation. But I did find a year-old article by him in which he writes, "We physicists are the only scientists who can say the word 'God' and not blush."[2]

I also found, on YouTube, an even older interview suggesting what he meant by those words.[3] In the interview, Dr. Kaku describes the way Albert Einstein thought about God: "the God of order, harmony, beauty, simplicity and elegance"[4]--the ultimate reason we find structure in the cosmos where there could have been chaos, and loveliness where there could have been ugliness. Since Dr. Kaku is an expert in cosmology (the study of the universe's origin and development), I suspect this is the kind of God he can talk about without blushing.

When the people who wrote the Bible looked at the heavens and the earth, they too saw structure and beauty:

- "Heaven is declaring God's glory," the psalm-singer rejoices; "the sky is proclaiming his handiwork" (Psalm 19:1).
- In Isaiah, God insists that God did not "create [the earth as] a wasteland but formed it as a habitation...I didn't say...'Seek me in chaos'" (45:18, 19).
- The Bible begins, in Genesis 1, with a highly structured poem about the highly structured world God made: a "supremely good" world (verse 31) where waters and land, trees and plants, birds and beasts, man and woman all exist in well-balanced harmony.

Scripture affirms that God *is* a God of order, harmony, elegance. But it also says more about God than scientists, even those who are religious, ever can.

Science cannot prove *or* disprove God's reality. Science is a powerful tool for observing and analyzing the natural world; it's indispensable for forming, testing, and refining ideas about how the world works. But no amount of natural structure observed or theorized by scientists leads to the inescapable, ironclad conclusion that an intelligent, intentional Creator exists (or doesn't), much less the God in whom we Christians believe.

The Apostles' Creed identifies God as "the Father Almighty." That phrase is partly about our belief that God is the "creator of heaven and earth" (although notice that the Creed doesn't give a blow-by-blow account of *how* God created; it simply states God *did*). But it's even more about our relationship to our (and everyone and everything else's) Creator. And this relationship means we *should* blush when we talk about God—not from embarrassment, but from love.

What Calling God "Father" Really Means

Christians call God "Father" because Jesus did, and told us to as well.

He taught his disciples, "Pray like this: Our Father who is in heaven..." (Matthew 6:9). Jesus wasn't dictating a specific set of words his followers must recite exactly as he spoke them every time they pray; he didn't wake up that morning and say, "Today I'll write 'The Lord's Prayer.'" He was showing his followers the attitude they should have when talking and listening to God. He was teaching them to talk with God not as a creature talking with the "creator of heaven and earth," but as a child talking with a parent. He was inviting them to experience the same kind of close, personal, loving relationship with God that he experienced.

Jesus wasn't the first person to talk about God as a father. The exact phrase "Father in heaven" isn't a name for God in the Old Testament, but Hebrew Scripture pictures God as the father of the people of Israel (for example, Deuteronomy 1:31; Jeremiah 31:9; Hosea 11:1-4) and, occasionally, as father on a more personal scale: "As a father has compassion for his children," the psalm-singer assures us, "so the LORD has compassion for those who fear him" (103:13 NRSV).

But by Jesus' time, the name "Father in heaven" had become one way Jewish rabbis identified God—less frequently than names like "King of the universe," but about a hundred uses of the phrase "Father in heaven" show up in rabbinic writings. "Upon whom can we rely?" asks one of these texts. The answer: "Upon our Father in Heaven."[5]

As a name for God, "Father in heaven" isn't without potential problems. For some people, it reinforces an unbiblical assumption that God is literally male—the Big Old Man on a king's throne in the sky, usually with a long white beard, often seen in old religious art.

For other people, the name associates God with human fathers in painful ways. Fathers who abuse, abandon, or simply don't pay enough attention to their kids can make it hard, if not impossible, for those kids to think about God as "the Father Almighty" at any age. How could anyone worship, let alone love, a bigger version of someone who let them down, made them angry, or scared and hurt them so much? How could anyone else tell them they must?

I think Jesus understands those kinds of concerns. I *know* he cares about the people who have them. His church should too. No one should be criticized or made to feel uncomfortable because they don't want to call God "Father."

But the church shouldn't lose "Father" as a name for God either. It connects us to biblical truth, historic tradition, and Jesus' own prayer life— but it also does something else. It shows us how God defines what the word *Father* means. We don't call God "Father in heaven" because God happens to remind us of the really great dad we have or wish we had on earth. It's the other way around: we know a human dad is really great when, and only when, he reminds us of God.

And the same goes for mothers, and brothers and sisters, and husbands and wives, and friends. We don't judge God by our human relationships, to see how well God measures up. We measure our human relationships by the standard God sets in God's relationship with us.

The God Who Exists—And Loves

"Father" is the only name in the Apostles' Creed, but that doesn't make it the only available or acceptable option. The Bible talks about and pictures God in many ways: as a mother (Deuteronomy 32:18; Isaiah 42:14; 49:15; 66:13), as a winged bird (Deuteronomy 32:11; Psalms 57:1; 91:4; Luke 13:34), as a rock (2 Samuel 23:3; Isaiah 44:8), as a tower (Psalm 61:3; Proverbs 18:10), and more. We need a variety of names and images for God.

And because proper Christian God-talk always begins in our actual experience of God, we can use new names and images if they highlight some quality of God we know is true because Jesus' life and ministry confirm it.

For example, on Sunday, September 16, 2001—five days after the terrorist attacks in New York, Washington, D.C., and Pennsylvania—Jesus' parables about a shepherd seeking a lost sheep and a woman hunting for a lost coin (Luke 15:1-10) were the assigned Gospel reading in many churches.[6] The horrific images of collapsing towers and burning buildings were still smoldering in so many people's eyes and minds…but scenes of brave first responders rushing toward the smoke and debris to look for trapped victims were also on TV and in hearts. That Sunday, I know that more than one preacher chose to talk about Jesus, not as the Good Shepherd, but as the Good Firefighter, the Good Police Officer, the Good Paramedic, who searches tirelessly for the lost in hopes of bringing them home in joy.

The Apostles' Creed doesn't offer any provable evidence of God from nature or any other source. It doesn't present any philosophical arguments for God's existence. And I wonder if that's because, at our core, we human beings aren't really as interested in the question "Does God exist?" as we are in the question "Does God exist *for me*? Does a God exist who cares about me? Does a God exist who can strengthen and support me when times are tough? Does a God exist who loves me as I am? Is there, out there, a God I can trust?"

Jesus' earliest followers met that God in him: the God whose deep, fierce love meant no distance was far enough to keep God from them. If they were to ascend to heaven, God would be there; if they were to descend to the grave, God would be there too (see Psalm 139:7-8). But they didn't have to go up or go down: in Jesus, God moved for and toward them (see Ephesians 4:9-10), entering the world as a humble servant whose service led him "to the point of death, even death on a cross" (Philippians 2:8). And after they encountered the risen Jesus, his friends came to realize, as the Apostle Paul wrote, that *nothing*, not even death, could ever separate them from God's love in Christ (see Romans 8:38-39).

That's God, the Father Almighty: the God who is and will do and will be whatever it takes to love me, to love you…the heavenly Father who "so loved the world that he gave his only Son, so that everyone who believes in him won't perish but will have eternal life" (John 3:16).

So tell me, are you blushing yet?

Some Questions to Think About

- How well do you think science and religion can complement each other? Do you agree that "[s]cience cannot prove *or* disprove God's reality"? Why?
- How comfortable are you with calling God "Father"? What other names for and images of God do you use in your prayers?
- How close is your relationship with God? How, if at all, has it changed over time?
- What about Jesus most clearly shows you that God exists for you and loves you?

REFLECT WITH SCRIPTURE

Read Exodus 2:23–3:15. As a baby, thanks to his mother's and sister's quick thinking, Moses escaped Pharaoh's plot to kill all the boys born among his Hebrew slaves. Moses was raised by Pharaoh's own daughter. As an adult, he murdered an Egyptian he saw beating an enslaved Hebrew man, then ran away to save his own life. The story in our Scripture takes place far away and many years later, after Moses has settled into his new life as a shepherd.

- Moses sees a bush that is burning but is not burned up. What does this "amazing sight" (verse 3) suggest about how God is and acts in the world?
- God tells Moses, "I am... Abraham's God, Isaac's God, and Jacob's God" (verse 6). How can knowing what God has done in the past help us recognize and believe in God in the present? How can that same knowledge hinder us when we're seeking God today?
- What does God's explanation to Moses in verses 7-10 tell us about who God is and what God does?
- In the ancient world, knowledge of a thing or being's name was believed to give you power over it. What does God's name (verse 14) tell us about God's freedom from human control?
- God assures Moses, "I'll be with you" (verse 12). How can people know God is with them today? How do you know God is with you?

- What does this story show us about what believing in God looks like in practical terms?

SUGGESTED ACTIVITIES

"Psalm 8 File"

Read Psalm 8. The psalm-singer sees God's wonderful works on earth and in heaven, and is moved that the Creator of all things still cares so much for human beings. Look through old issues of nature and astronomy magazines, or look online, for images that impress you with the beauty of God's creation. Clip the pictures and save them in a file folder (real or virtual). Use these images this week as aids for meditation and prayer.

An "Oldie-But-a-Goodie"

Find and listen to the song "One of Us" (written by Eric Bazilian, originally sung by Joan Osborne in 1995).

- How do you react to the questions it asks about God?
- Do you think the song takes belief in God seriously? Why or why not?
- Does the song prompt you to rethink how you picture God for yourself? Why or why not?

Faith and Film

In *Bruce Almighty* (2003), God (Morgan Freeman) offers Bruce (Jim Carrey), a local TV personality who's unhappy with his life, the chance "to do God's job better." (Suggested sample: Bruce meets God and discovers how much God knows about him, at 0:26:13–0:32:29.)

- What do you like best about this movie's depiction of God? What do you like least? Why?
- What about God in this film do you think agrees with how the Bible presents God? What doesn't?
- Would Jesus recognize God in this movie as his and our "Father in heaven"? Why or why not?

WHAT DO YOU BELIEVE?

A new thought I had about God in this session:

_____

A question I still have about God after this session:

_____

One thing I want others to know I believe about God:

_____

2.

JESUS CHRIST

I believe in Jesus Christ, his only Son, our Lord,
who was conceived by the Holy Spirit,
born of the Virgin Mary,
suffered under Pontius Pilate,
was crucified, died, and was buried;
he descended to the dead.
On the third day he rose again;
he ascended into heaven,
is seated at the right hand of the Father,
and will come again to judge the living
and the dead.

PRAY A PSALM

I won't die—no, I will live
and declare what the LORD has done.
Yes, the LORD definitely disciplined me,
but he didn't hand me over to death.

Open the gates of righteousness for me
    so I can come in and give thanks to the LORD!
This is the LORD's *gate;*
    those who are righteous enter through it.

I thank you because you answered me,
    because you were my saving help.
The stone rejected by the builders
    is now the main foundation stone!
This has happened because of the LORD;
    it is astounding in our sight!
This is the day the LORD *acted;*
    we will rejoice and celebrate in it!

—*Psalm 118:17-24*

GET THE CONVERSATION ROLLING

Roll a six-sided die and answer the corresponding question from the list below.

1. My favorite Bible story about Jesus is…because…
2. What TV series would Jesus want to binge watch on Netflix?
3. What social media would Jesus use?
4. One thing the Bible doesn't tell us about Jesus that I want to know is…
5. What one word or image best sums up all Jesus is and does for you?
6. What I most want to hear Jesus say to me is…

CONSIDER THE CREED

Spellbound by Stories

In 1977, when I was five years old, my parents took me to see *Star Wars*. It was the first story I ever fell in love with.

The action-packed, eye-popping epic of good versus evil in outer space grabbed hold of my imagination and, almost forty years later, still hasn't let go. After only two viewings in the theater, I could—and did—recite whole stretches of the movie scene by scene, sometimes line by line, for well-intentioned grown-ups who asked (and probably regretted it), "So what's that movie about?" But how could I help myself? *Star Wars* was an amazing story, and I was not reluctant in the least to talk (and talk, and talk) about it!

What's the first story *you* ever fell in love with? Maybe yours was *Star Wars* too, although your first exposure to that galaxy far, far away is more likely to have come through one of the prequels or *The Clone Wars* animated series. Or maybe you're a devoted Harry Potter fan who grew up going to midnight release parties at bookstores whenever a new novel in the series arrived.

Maybe the first story you loved wasn't a story most people noticed: a movie or TV show that, to this day, no one else seems to care much about, or a book from your school library that you could check out whenever you wanted because nobody else ever did.

Maybe the first story you loved was a true story. You might have enjoyed hearing an older relative tell tales from your family tree, or a grandparent remember the times your parents got into trouble when *they* were kids—those stories are often real winners!

We're hardwired for stories. Some other species appear to use language, but, as far as we can tell, only human beings are storytellers. And when we're telling *good* stories, we're doing more than entertaining one another (though the best stories are always entertaining). We're communicating something of value and importance. Even if we're not aware of it, we tell stories to put what really matters into words.

That's why good stories are a kind of magic. They keep us spellbound. As J. R. R. Tolkien wrote, "Small wonder that *spell* means both a story told, and a formula of power over living men."[1] Humans keep falling under the spell of stories because the good ones, the great ones, give us powerful insights into what we and the world are all about.

The Greatest Story Partly Told

That's why the second section of the Apostles' Creed, the section about Jesus, has always been my favorite. Unlike the rest of the Creed, important as all of it is, this part tells a story.

No, not in as much detail as you might expect. When you compare what the Apostles' Creed tells us about Jesus with what we learn in the New Testament's four Gospels, you might be surprised at what gets left out:

- "Conceived by the Holy Spirit" (or "Ghost," as the King James Bible has it) and "born of the Virgin Mary"—What about angels, shepherds, wise men? What about Joseph? A Christmas pageant with only the Creed as source material would be pretty short!
- "Suffered under Pontius Pilate"—Apart from Mary and Jesus himself, the Roman governor of Judea is the only person from Jesus' life named in the Apostles' Creed. No Simon Peter. No Mary Magdalene. No Mary and Martha. No Nicodemus, or Lazarus, or Thomas. (And again, what about Joseph?) So many people loved and followed Jesus, why does the Creed name *Pilate*, of all people, the man who sentenced Jesus to death?
- "Was crucified, died, and was buried"—Why does the Creed jump directly from Jesus' birth to his death? Where are the stories of his wisdom and compassion, his power and love? The people he healed, the parables he preached, the stormy seas he calmed, the dead he brought back to life! An old hymn implores, "Tell me the stories of Jesus I love to hear"[2]—but you'll have to hear those stories from some source other than the Creed.
- "On the third day he rose again..."—You might think here, at least, the Creed would want to elaborate a little. After all, in the earliest known written account of the first Easter, the Apostle Paul points to many people who saw the risen, living Jesus (1 Corinthians 15:3-8). But the Creed contains nothing about joyful meetups on the road to Emmaus, or in the upper room, or by the shores of the Sea of Galilee.

In the English translation of the Creed we're using, Jesus' entire life—from his miraculous conception to his promised return—takes up just 264 characters. That's not enough to fill up even two tweets! If you handed in this part of the Creed to your Language Arts teacher as a story, he or she would hand it right back, probably with a note scrawled in red ink: "Need more detail; tell me more!"

What's in the Name?

Actually, the Creed tells more of Jesus' story than we might realize, simply by identifying its main character as "Jesus Christ, [God's] only Son, our Lord."

"Jesus"

Although most English-speaking Christians think of only one "Jesus" when they hear the name, it was a common one among first-century Jews, just as it is in Spanish- and Portuguese-speaking cultures today.[3] In the Hebrew and Aramaic of Jesus' day (Jesus spoke Aramaic), his name was "Yeshua." As of 2008, archaeologists had discovered seventy-one tombs of Jewish men named Yeshua who lived in Judea around that time.[4] So Jesus' name is—only in this sense—nothing special. It emphasizes how "ordinary," to all appearances, he actually was.

The name also reminds us he *was* Jewish, a fact many Christians who aren't of Jewish descent tend to forget or overlook. Too often, the Christian church has forgotten what the Apostle Paul taught: that God has generously adopted non-Jewish believers into the people of Israel through Jesus. God has freely chosen to make them one branch of Abraham's holy, chosen family tree—so they shouldn't "brag like [they're] better than the other branches" (Romans 11:18). The church's frequent failure to remember Jesus' Jewishness has contributed, indirectly and directly, to terrible fear of and violence toward Jews, including the Holocaust. Christians, who have been commanded to love our neighbors, cannot support hatred of *any* ethnic or religious group, but especially not Jews, who are our own family through Jesus.

The name "Jesus" appears in Hebrew Scripture as both "Yeshua" and, more often, as "Yehoshua"—in English, "Joshua." (So in its longer form, "Jesus" turns out to be not so uncommon in English-speaking cultures after all.) You probably recognize that name, if not from Sunday school lessons then maybe from the old spiritual about walls that came tumblin' down. Joshua, Moses' assistant, led the Israelites into Canaan after Moses died. By guiding them to the Promised Land and spearheading their battles against enemies, Joshua acted as a savior for the Israelites. Appropriately, the name Joshua—Yehoshua, Yeshua, Jesus—means "God is salvation."[5]

As God saved the Israelites through Joshua, bringing them to a new home and defeating their human foes, God has saved all God's people through Jesus, opening the way to our true home and defeating our cosmic foes of sin, evil, and death. If the Creed called this man nothing but "Jesus," we'd know a lot about him from only his name!

"Christ"

But the Creed identifies this Jesus further, because much more must be said. He is "Jesus Christ." No, Christ was not a last name you'd find in the Nazareth phone book! It's a title, the Greek translation of the Hebrew word *messiah*, which means "anointed one."

We don't see many literal anointings in modern American society. You may see people being anointed with oil in your church at baptisms or confirmations, or when someone is sick, as a form of prayer (see James 5:14-15). But we do still hear about metaphorical "anointings." Consider this item from the *New York Times'* sports pages: "With another playoff-less season concluding in Indiana on Tuesday night, Phil Jackson has the always contentious chore of anointing yet another Knicks head coach."[6] The ceremony may be rare, but its meaning has survived: to be anointed is to be chosen to do a particular job, set apart from other people for a special purpose.

In ancient Israel, anointing with oil symbolized God's selection of someone for a special task. Prophets, God's human messengers, could be anointed (1 Kings 19:16; Psalm 105:15). Priests, who served as "go-betweens" for God and God's people, were anointed (Exodus 28:41; Leviticus 8:12). Kings were anointed too. When the prophet Samuel anointed both of Israel's first two kings, Saul (1 Samuel 10:1-9) and David (1 Samuel 16:12-13), God's spirit filled them, empowering them for their God-given work of ruling.

Jesus' followers came to believe he had been chosen by God and filled with God's spirit for work that resembled all three of these ancient offices. In his teaching and preaching, he was like a prophet, speaking God's message with authority. In sacrificing his own life to save people from sin, he was like a priest, offering himself to God on the "altar" of the cross. And in his claim to "all authority in heaven and on earth" (Matthew 28:18), his promised return to rule all things in glory and his present guiding of his church through the Holy Spirit, he was and is like a king. For all these reasons, they called Jesus the Messiah, the Christ (Mark 8:29).

(*Fun fact*: According to U.S. census data from 2010, there are seven people named "Jesus Christ" in the United States.[7] People having fun on the questionnaire? Parents putting unusually high expectations on their kid? Legal name changes made for religious or rebellious reasons? You've got to wonder!)

God's "Only Son, Our Lord"

We've seen that Scripture mentions other "messiahs," other anointed ones. Even Cyrus, the non-Jewish, Persian king who lived about five centuries before Jesus, is called messiah: the prophet Isaiah believed God chose Cyrus to conquer the Babylonian Empire and let its captives, including Jewish exiles, return to their homelands (Isaiah 45:1). So what makes *this* messiah, Jesus, different from the rest? Part of the Creed's answer is that Jesus is God's "only Son."

Like "messiah," "Son of God" was an idea familiar in Israel's history. Israel's kings, who never claimed to be anything but fully human, were called "sons of God." God promised King David, for example, that one of David's descendants, Solomon, would rule after him and build the temple David never did: "I will be a father to him, and he will be a son to me" (2 Samuel 7:14; see also 1 Chronicles 28:6). And Psalm 2, which scholars believe was sung to celebrate a new king's coronation, includes this declaration from God: "I hereby appoint my king on Zion, my holy mountain!... You are my son, today I have become your father" (verses 6-7). According to Matthew, Mark, and Luke, Jesus heard similar words when John baptized him. Jesus "saw heaven splitting open" and the Spirit settling on him "like a dove," and heard God say, "You are my Son, whom I dearly love; in you I find happiness" (Mark 1:10-11).

As we saw in the first session, Jesus understood himself to be connected to God in an extremely close and personal way. We don't know when he first fully understood this relationship—he must have had at least glimmerings of it by age twelve, when he told Mary and Joseph, who were looking all over Jerusalem for him, that they should have known he would be in the Temple, his "Father's house" (Luke 2:49)—but once John baptized him, Jesus was ready to start doing what he believed his Father had sent him to do (see, for example, John 4:34; 5:19; 8:28-29).

But if, as we also saw in our first session, Jesus invited everyone to relate to God as a child relates to a parent, why does the Creed call Jesus God's "only" Son?

It's important to remember the Creed isn't trying to say anything new. Instead, it's attempting to honor and preserve the earliest Christians' experience of Jesus. After his resurrection, looking back on all that Jesus had said and done, they became convinced the God of Israel had been present in him in a unique way. They could not explain it; they could only affirm it. When they called Jesus "Son of God," they were trying to put this incredibly close connection between Jesus and God into words—*identifying* the two of them without *confusing* the two of them.

Jesus was already being called God's Son by the time Paul wrote his letters, starting only twenty years or so after the Crucifixion; so the apostle can say, for instance, that he lives "by the faithfulness of God's Son, who loved me and gave himself for me" (Galatians 2:20). Similarly, the Gospels include references to Jesus as the Son of God (for example, Matthew 16:16), especially the Gospel of John, in which Jesus repeatedly stresses his closeness to God. "Whoever has seen me has seen the Father" he says. "I am in the Father and the Father is in me" (14:9-10). He even says, "I and the Father are one" (10:30)—meaning not that they are one and the same person, but that he and God are utterly united in what they will and what they do.

No devout Jew (and Jesus was) would ever dare claim to be God. No devout Jew (and all of Jesus' first followers were) would ever dare worship a human being as God. But Jesus' disciples found no response *except* worship adequately expressed their love for and gratitude to him. They called him "Lord," a title only the God of Israel could command (Deuteronomy 6:4), but had no fear they were committing blasphemy when they did. Paul wrote that "no one can say, 'Jesus is Lord,' except by the Holy Spirit" (1 Corinthians 12:3). In Jesus, these first believers found themselves face to face with God the Lord as they never had in anyone else. He was uniquely related to God.

And they believed *their* relationships to God came from and depended upon this unique Son of God. John the Evangelist wrote that "to all who received [Jesus], who believed in his name, he gave power to become children of God" (1:12 NRSV). In the broadest sense—that all life comes from God— we are all God's children, and we are brothers and sisters to one another by virtue of being humans created in God's image. But a new, deeper, and closer relationship with God is possible for those who trust in Jesus. The Letter to the Hebrews pictures Jesus as our big brother, bringing us into God's presence and saying, "Here I am with the children whom God has given to me" (2:13).

Maybe you can see why the church felt it had to explain all this more fully as time passed, not only to sort things out for itself but also defend itself against critics. The doctrine of the Trinity (fully developed by the fourth century) and the official definition of Jesus' full humanity and full divinity (fully developed by the fifth) use precise and accurate language to explain God's presence in Jesus—but it is language borrowed from ancient Greek philosophy, not from the Bible. The doctrines are important, but they're one more step removed from the first Christians' actual experience of Jesus.

Restricting itself to biblical language, the Apostles' Creed doesn't answer all our questions about Jesus' relationship to God. But its names and titles for him tell us all we ultimately need to know. He has a relationship with God that no one else can claim, but which everyone else can share as a gift through him when they trust in him as Savior, the one chosen by God to rule us as Lord.

His Story Becomes Our Story

So why does the Apostles' Creed tell Jesus' story the way it does?

When I read its words about Jesus, I imagine some breathless early believer telling the tale with excitement and urgency—the way I told the story of *Star Wars* when I was a kid, except the Creed storyteller knows how to stay focused on the big picture!

The Creed tells Jesus' story in broad strokes so we don't miss the truth that it's the story of God's unique intervention in human history. This miraculous life unlike any other—"Jesus Christ, [God's] only Son, our Lord," God's immediate presence in human form appeared at a specific point in human history. He was supernaturally conceived but was born to a real, identifiable woman. He really suffered and died a real death on the watch of a real, identifiable Roman governor, but he was raised from death and is coming again.

You can't help noticing the intersections of heaven and earth, time and eternity, humanity and divinity in the way the Creed tells Jesus' story. It's a story of divine intervention, but, unlike so many ancient stories of gods, this one is no myth. It took place in our world, not some "once upon a time." As the Apostle Paul once testified, these things "didn't happen secretly or in some out-of-the-way place" (Acts 26:26). Christian faith stakes everything on the belief that, two thousand years ago, in Jesus of Nazareth, God entered our world as one of us in order to save us and it.

That's a story that communicates a message of value and importance. *That's* a story that puts into words something that really matters. *That's* a story that tells us who we are and what we are all about. Jesus' movement from life to death to new life becomes, by God's love and grace, *our* movement. As the Letter to the Ephesians says, God has raised us to new life together with Christ, claiming us "for good works, which God prepared beforehand to be our way of life" (verse 10; see Ephesians 2:1-10 NRSV). *That's* a story worth falling in love with.

Even the authors of the Gospels realized that no one can say everything that could be said about Jesus when telling his story. John the Evangelist concluded that if someone tried to record all the things Jesus did, "I imagine the world itself wouldn't have enough room for the scrolls that would be written" (21:25). Any telling of Jesus' story must be selective. The Apostles' Creed, laser-focused as it is on the basic facts of Jesus' story, may seem *too* selective to some people. But generations of believers worldwide have found it a useful and trustworthy summary of who Jesus is and why he matters. It has helped *them* focus on the heart of the gospel.

Some Questions to Think About

- What's your all-time favorite story? What about it appeals to you?
- If someone asked you to tell them the story of Jesus for the first time, how would you tell it?

- Of the four names or titles the Apostles' Creed uses for Jesus—"Jesus," "Christ," "God's only Son," "Lord"—which one do you find the most meaningful, and why?
- Do you find any of these names or titles difficult? If so, why?
- What other names for or titles of Jesus have you found meaningful?
- If you were asked to add one sentence to the Creed about Jesus' life between his birth and death, what would you write?
- How have you experienced the movement of Jesus' story—from death to life, from earth to heaven—in your life because of him?

REFLECT WITH SCRIPTURE

Read Luke 8:22-25.

- What about Jesus is shown by the fact that he is able to sleep during the storm?
- What is significant about the fact that the disciples call him "Master"?
- What does Jesus' command of the storm show about him? (Be sure also to read Genesis 1:1-9; Job 38:8-11.)
- What has been a "storm" for you in which you've heard Jesus ask, "Where is your faith?" What was your answer?

Read 1 Corinthians 15:1-11.

- Why does Paul think his readers need this summary of the message he preaches?
- How is this summary story of Jesus like and unlike the story the Apostles' Creed tells?
- How does knowing the community of faith's story help Paul understand his personal story?
- When have the stories you've received from the church helped you know Jesus, yourself, and others better?

SUGGESTED ACTIVITIES

Singing the Story of Jesus

Look through your congregation's hymnal or songbook, or search the web, for songs that tell the story of Jesus' life. Look for songs both old and new.

Sing or listen to several examples. What do these songs have in common? How are they different? If you were going to write a song about the story of Jesus, what would you be sure to include, and what might you feel you could leave out? (If you're feeling especially creative, go ahead and try writing and performing your song!)

Picturing the Story of Jesus

Gather as many examples as you can of art that tells Jesus' story. Look at illustrated Bibles, old Sunday school or vacation Bible school materials, and the Internet. Try to find pictures that represent a variety of time periods and art styles. Prepare a "gallery" that displays the art together. What common subjects do you see? Which artwork is most interesting or unusual, and why? How does the art prompt you to think about Jesus' story in new ways? What are the advantages and limitations of telling Jesus' story through images?

Biblical "Creeds"

The New Testament includes several creed-like statements of faith. Choose two of the following texts. Compare and contrast them. What important things does each one tell us about the story of Jesus? How are they similar and different in what they emphasize, and why might differences exist? What questions, if any, do these statements leave unanswered? Why is it important to realize that Scripture contains more than one "creed" about Jesus?

- 1 Corinthians 15:1-11
- Ephesians 2:1-10
- Philippians 2:1-11
- Colossians 1:15-20
- 1 Timothy 2:5-6
- 2 Timothy 2:5-13

Comic Strip Creed

Draw a comic strip in which you illustrate each phrase about Jesus' story from the Apostles' Creed as a panel in a comic strip. Display or reproduce your comic strip for others in your congregation to see.

Color-Code the Creed

Create a clean copy of the section about Jesus' story from the Apostles' Creed. Using red, green, and yellow crayons, markers, or highlighters, mark each phrase as follows: Green = "I have no trouble believing this about Jesus"; Yellow = "I still have some questions about this"; Red = "No way can I believe this about Jesus!" Compare your color-coded creed with someone else's. (This could be done anonymously, by having a group leader gather all sheets and tallying the results for each phrase.) Discuss the activity by talking with someone who responded differently than you did to a particular phrase—for example, if you colored one phrase yellow, talk to someone who colored the same phrase green. Remember: when we recite the Creed, we are reciting the historic faith of the church—but that doesn't mean we can't wonder about and explore it further. Who would you trust to help you answer any questions about the Creed that you have?

Faith and Film

Christians and non-Christians alike have been fascinated by what the Bible doesn't tell us about Jesus' story, especially in the years between Bethlehem and the beginning of his public ministry. Watch *The Young Messiah* (2016), or at least the opening sequence (to about 0:12:28). This movie imagines Jesus' life at age seven. The opening sequence shows the young Jesus performing a (nonbiblical) miracle.

- Do you think Jesus, as depicted in this movie, is consistent with Jesus as we read about him in Scripture? Why or why not?
- Why do you think people are fascinated by what Scripture doesn't tell us about Jesus?
- Do you think movies and stories like *The Young Messiah* can encourage or nurture faith in Jesus, or do they distract from it? Why?

WHAT DO YOU BELIEVE?

A new thought I had about Jesus in this session:

_____

A question I still have about Jesus after this session:

_____

One thing I want others to know I believe about Jesus:

_____

3.

THE HOLY SPIRIT

I believe in the Holy Spirit…

PRAY A PSALM

Lord, you have done so many things!
　　You made them all so wisely!
The earth is full of your creations!…
All your creations wait for you
　　to give them their food on time.
When you give it to them, they gather it up;
　　when you open your hand, they are filled completely full!
But when you hide your face, they are terrified;
　　when you take away their breath,
　　they die and return to dust.
When you let loose your breath, they are created,
　　and you make the surface of the ground brand-new again.
　　　　　　　　　　　　　—Psalm 104:24, 27-30

GET THE CONVERSATION ROLLING

Roll a six-sided die and answer the corresponding question from the list below.

1. What do you do when you need to feel energized?
2. When you hear the term "Holy Spirit," what immediately comes to mind?
3. What's something you've heard about the Holy Spirit that confuses you?
4. What's a symbol for the Holy Spirit that is meaningful to you?
5. Who is someone you know or know about whom you think is spiritually gifted, and why?
6. What is one of your spiritual gifts?

CONSIDER THE CREED

What Gives You Wings?

You've seen the commercials—of *course* you have, because this company *really* knows how to market its product—and you've heard the slogan. The idea is that what's being sold will make you more alert, more focused, more creative, more adventurous. Whatever you're about to do, from studying to extreme skydiving, you'll do it better because "Red Bull gives you wings!"

What Red Bull actually gives you is caffeine. A twelve-ounce can has 114 mg of it.[1] That's more than is in a twelve-ounce can of Coca-Cola (between 23–35 mg),[2] but less than is in twelve ounces of coffee (a "tall" regular at Starbucks, for example, has 260 mg).[3] Caffeine increases heart rate and blood pressure, so it can make us more alert and attentive, at least for a while. But the more we drink, the more our bodies get used to it, and the more of it we need to get the same feeling. Too much caffeine can also make people feel jittery, get an upset stomach, or have trouble sleeping.[4]

Energy drinks such as Red Bull are incredibly popular (and profitable; the energy drink market is forecast to be worth almost *$62 billion* by 2021).[5] Maybe you like them; just over a third of youth ages twelve to nineteen regularly drink energy drinks, according to one study published by heart doctors in 2015. But while those doctors concluded that a single eight-ounce can per day is probably safe for healthy adolescents, drinking too many energy drinks carries some real risks, up to and including death (especially if combined with alcohol or other drugs, as increasing evidence suggests they often are).[6]

There are plenty of healthier ways to energize ourselves. A balanced diet, regular exercise, a good night's sleep—these are some tried-and-true methods. But we human beings have gotten really good at looking for shortcuts! And that's a major reason that energy drinks sell so well. Power in a can! Liquid strength that lifts us up so we can become the best versions of ourselves we can be.

The Apostles' Creed is silent on the subject of Red Bull (duh), but it does talk about *real* power, *real* strength, *real* force. The Creed names the source of spiritual energy that really does sustain and change us—not just for the short term, but for the long haul. "I believe," says the Creed, "in the Holy Spirit."

The Spirit of Jesus

Upfront admission: It's risky to talk about the Holy Spirit as energy. Energy is an impersonal thing. Energy can't love, or comfort, or guide, or inspire. And talk about "divine energy" sounds suspiciously like the Force from the *Star Wars* movies—in wise old Ben Kenobi's words, "an energy field created by all living things" that "surrounds us and penetrates us. It binds the galaxy together."

So we have to remember, always, that the Apostles' Creed summarizes the early Church's *experience* of Jesus. His earliest followers found, after his resurrection, that even when he was no longer with them physically—after, as the Creed says, "he ascended into heaven"—he was still with them spiritually. Matthew's Gospel even ends with Jesus promising his disciples, "I myself will be with you every day until the end of this present age" (28:20). No, Jesus' followers couldn't walk and talk and eat with him as they did during those three years in and around Galilee. But they felt and knew they were, somehow, walking and talking and even (in the meal of bread and wine he commanded them to celebrate) eating with him just the same.

So the Holy Spirit is not an impersonal energy field, let alone one we generate simply by being alive. Some Christians call the Spirit "him" and "he," others "her" and "she," but the important thing is to avoid calling the Spirit "it"! The Spirit is a *person*, not a *thing*.

And the Spirit is not some vague and shadowy person, as the older language of "Holy Ghost" can suggest to some modern ears. The Holy Spirit is Jesus' spirit. The Holy Spirit is Jesus with us, on this side of Easter—still loving us, comforting us, guiding us, inspiring us. The influential twentieth-century theologian Karl Barth wrote:

> "[T]he Holy Spirit is nothing other than the relationship between Christ and us. Wherever this relationship . . . becomes a fact in [people's] lives, he is present and acting. This reality of the Holy Spirit is the simplest thing on earth, while it remains of course the greatest mystery."[7]

Divine Energy

All the same, talking about the Holy Spirit as energy appeals to me because, throughout both the Old and New Testaments, the Spirit is energetically active: flowing, blowing, pouring, pulsing through the world and through people in order to get divine work done!

At the beginning of all things and all time, we see the Spirit, God's creative energy, at work. As God brought light out of darkness, order out of disorder, and life out of lifelessness, "God's wind swept over the waters" (Genesis 1:2). The Hebrew word for "wind," *ruach* (ROO-awk), can also be translated into English, just as accurately, as "breath" or "spirit." In the New Testament, the Greek word *pneuma* (NOO-ma) also means all three things. The Holy Spirit is God's wind, God's breath. The Spirit gives existence and life. The Spirit opens up life-filled futures.

That's why it makes sense that the first time the Apostles' Creed mentions the Holy Spirit is in connection with Jesus' birth. You'll remember it says that Jesus was "conceived by the Holy Spirit, [and] born of the Virgin Mary."

Jesus' conception is the only miracle from his earthly life, other than the Resurrection, mentioned in the Creed. For some people, that fact makes it a nonnegotiable item—something you *must* believe in order to qualify as

Christian. Others disagree. They point out, for example, that if the Apostle Paul knew about the circumstances of Jesus' conception and birth, he never mentioned it; all he ever says about it is that God's Son was "born through a woman, and born under the [Jewish] Law" (Galatians 4:4).

Though I think God could arrange Jesus' supernatural conception (how hard could it be for the Creator of everything to bypass normal human biology?), I don't think the Creed is some theological pop quiz: "Believe at least 75 percent of these things, or you flunk out!" The Creed lays out what the ancient church *as a whole* believed, whether or not every single Christian agreed with every single item. And the ancient church, as a whole, talked about the Holy Spirit as the giver of Jesus' life in order to highlight the Spirit's role as the divine energy that sparks and sustains all life.

The Holy Spirit, Hard at Work

After the Apostles' Creed mentions the Spirit a second time, it moves on to mention a lot of other, seemingly unrelated things: the church, forgiveness of sins, our future lives with God. . . . I've sometimes heard this part of the Creed called "the kitchen sink paragraph"! We'll talk about all these items in more detail later; for now, think about the Holy Spirit as being involved in them all.

Start with the church. The Book of Acts makes it clear the church's life depends on the Holy Spirit's activity. Jesus' first followers are a group of scared and silent individuals until, on the Day of Pentecost, "a sound from heaven like the howling of a fierce wind" and "what seemed to be individual flames of fire" signal the Spirit's arrival (2:2-3). Then these women and men become a unified group of God's bold and outspoken messengers, doing deeds of power and telling anyone and everyone who'll listen, "God has made this Jesus . . . both Lord and Christ" (2:36). As the Spirit created light and life in the beginning, and as the Spirit brought about Jesus' birth, so the Spirit gave birth to Jesus' church, and continues to support and strengthen it.

Then think about the forgiveness of our sins. We tend to think about Jesus forgiving us, but Scripture also credits the pardon we receive to the Holy Spirit. In Psalm 51, for instance, the psalm-singer asks God for "a new, faithful spirit deep inside . . . please don't take your holy spirit away from me" (verses 10-11). It's almost a prayer for a spirit transplant: "Take away my sinful spirit, God, and fill me with your Holy Spirit instead." And the Apostle Paul says God's love "has been poured out in our hearts through the Holy Spirit, who has been given to us" (Romans 5:5). So while we believe Jesus' death brings us forgiveness, we also believe the Spirit helps us receive and experience that forgiveness. It's one more way the Spirit creates life: we were like dead people because of sin, but have now been forgiven and brought to life with Christ (see Ephesians 2:1-5).

And the Holy Spirit makes our future lives with God possible. Paul says God will raise us from the dead through the same Spirit through whom God raised Jesus from the dead—the same Spirit who lives in us right now (see Romans 8:11). We believe that "the life everlasting" isn't something that is "on hold" until we die: it begins here and now, in this earthly life. "This is eternal life," Jesus prayed, "to know you, the only true God, and Jesus Christ whom you sent" (John 17:3). The Holy Spirit empowers us to know God and Jesus, and to begin a life in their presence now that will continue and be made perfect after we die.

Spiritual Gifts

The Holy Spirit is God's gift to the whole church. The Spirit is also God's gift to every individual Christian. We don't all experience the Spirit's presence in the same way; as Paul told the believers in Corinth, "There are different spiritual gifts but the same Spirit...and there are different activities but the same God who produces all of them in everyone" (1 Corinthians 12:4, 6). But we believe the Spirit does give every Christian gifts to use for serving our neighbors and praising God.

A Google search I just ran for "spiritual gifts test" returned about 928,000 results! My hunch is spiritual gifts are better discerned over time, not determined by a quiz score. Look back over your life so far and think about times when you've felt especially energized for serving God and your neighbor. What were the circumstances? What, specifically and practically, were you doing? What results did you see? If you start to see a pattern developing, you may be seeing where your spiritual gifts are.

On the other hand, it's not always so simple! Scripture shows us the Spirit pushing plenty of people outside their comfort zones in order to do God's work and spread God's message. Even Jesus! After he was baptized by John, the Spirit immediately pushed him out into the wilderness to face temptations (Mark 1:12-13). Maybe you remember times you felt pushed into unknown, even unpleasant circumstances, a situation you'd never really choose again gladly, but you ended up helping someone while you were there. Or maybe you've been trying to make a positive difference about an urgent need in your community for a long time and haven't seen many, if any, results. These, too, may be signs of your spiritual gifts—don't dismiss them too quickly.

It's important to talk with other Christians—including older, more spiritually mature Christians—about what your gifts may be. Your gifts may or may not be quickly apparent, but you have them, because God has given you the Spirit in your baptism.

The Holy Spirit, the Spirit of Jesus, is at work in and around you right now, to make you holy...to love, comfort, guide, and inspire you...to transform you into the best version of yourself that you can possibly be, the person God created you to be. The Spirit is energizing you to love and serve your neighbors, to strengthen the body of Christ, in a way that no one else can in exactly the same way.

That's the energizing truth! That good news gives us wings!

Some Questions to Think About

- Where, how, and in whom do you see the Holy Spirit active today?
- How does identifying the Holy Spirit as Jesus' Spirit keep us from thinking about the Spirit in ways that are too abstract or mysterious?
- What do you think your spiritual gifts might be? Who do you (or could you) talk to in order to discover your gifts more clearly?
- Why is it important to remember that God gives us the Spirit so we can serve others and strengthen the church?

REFLECT WITH SCRIPTURE

Read Luke 4:14-30. These verses are Luke's account of the first sermon Jesus preached in his public ministry, and its aftermath, in Nazareth, the village where Jesus grew up.

- Why do you think Jesus chooses to read these verses?
- Based on these verses, how would you describe the Holy Spirit's work and priorities?
- Compare Isaiah 61:1-2 with what Jesus reads in Nazareth. What differences do you notice? What do these differences suggest to you about Jesus and his mission?
- Why does the congregation in Nazareth stop admiring Jesus (verse 22) and become so angry with him that they want to kill him (verses 28-29)?
- What do the stories from Israel's past that Jesus tells suggest about where and through whom the Holy Spirit can act?
- How did Jesus do the things he read about in Isaiah? How is Jesus' Spirit leading and empowering Christians to do these things today?

SUGGESTED ACTIVITIES

Research the Spirit in Scripture

Using a Bible search program or a Bible concordance, locate and read a passage about the Spirit from each of these categories: (1) an Old Testament story; (2) Old Testament poetry (psalm or a poetic text from a prophet); (3) a New Testament letter. What do these texts say about the Holy Spirit (or "Spirit of the Lord")? What similarities or differences do you notice in the Spirit, as discussed in these passages? What questions about the Spirit do these texts raise? If you had to choose one word to describe the Spirit that could apply to all the passages, what word would you choose?

Spirit Symbols

Two common symbols for the Holy Spirit in Christian art include a dove (because Jesus saw the Spirit descend on him as a dove when he was baptized) and fire (because the Spirit appeared as flames at Pentecost). Go around your church building looking for these or other symbols of the Spirit. If possible, snap digital photos and prepare a slideshow set to music you think communicates something about the Spirit. What new symbols for the Spirit would you suggest, and why?

Fruit (of the Spirit) Salad

Read Galatians 5:22-23. The Apostle Paul identifies nine "fruits of the Spirit," qualities that characterize the lives of those who live in relationship with Jesus Christ. What are they? What does each one mean to you? How do you see the members of your congregation displaying these qualities? Talk about these questions with others as you work together to make a fruit salad using nine types of fruit (fresh and/or frozen, depending on the season) to represent the nine qualities. Serve your fruit salad to others in your congregation.

WHAT DO YOU BELIEVE?

A new thought I had about the Holy Spirit in this session:

_____

A question I still have about the Holy Spirit after this session:

_____

One thing I want others to know I believe about the Holy Spirit:

_____

4.

THE CHURCH AND THE COMMUNION OF SAINTS

I believe in...
> *the holy catholic church,*
> *the communion of saints...*

PRAY A PSALM

Look at how good and pleasing it is
> *when families live together as one!*
It is like expensive oil poured over the head,
> *running down onto the beard—*
>> *Aaron's beard!—*
> *which extended over the collar of his robes.*
It is like the dew on Mount Hermon
> *streaming down onto the mountains of Zion,*
> *because it is there that the* LORD *has commanded the blessing:*
> *everlasting life.*

—Psalm 133

GET THE CONVERSATION ROLLING

Roll a six-sided die and answer the corresponding question from the list below.

1. What "better offer," if it came your way, would keep you from going to church next Sunday?
2. Name one thing you really like about your church.
3. Name one thing you really dislike about your church.
4. Do you think most Americans today have a positive or a negative view of the church? Why?
5. How many different churches in your community can you name?
6. If you had to choose one word to describe your church, what would it be?

CONSIDER THE CREED

A "Skip Sunday" From Church

When I was a teen, the only Sunday I can remember not going to church with my family was the morning after I'd caused a car accident.

No, I wasn't laid up in traction, thankfully! And nobody in the other car got hurt, either. I was a high school senior and still relatively new behind the wheel. I'd misjudged how much time I had to make a left turn before the oncoming car caught up to me. It was scary for the folks in the other car, scary *and* humiliating for me, and expensive for my parents. Still, things could have turned out much worse.

But the whole experience rattled me enough that my mom let me sleep in that Sunday morning. I woke up to an empty house and a few extra, unexpected hours to do whatever I wanted.

And you know what?

I found I kind of liked it!

I could watch whatever I wanted on TV. I could take as long to eat breakfast as I cared to. And I didn't have to put on a shirt, tie, and slacks. Sure, the circumstances of my "skip day" from church were less than ideal, but I appreciated for the first time why so many people look forward to leisurely Sunday mornings.

Getting Beyond "Going to Church"

According to recent research, 78 percent of American high school and college students say they believe in God, but only 41 percent say they go to weekly religious services.[1]

 Incidentally, those numbers mean your generation goes to church more than your elders do! Only 21 percent of your parents' generation and only 26 percent of your grandparents' generation report weekly church attendance. So if you ever hear a grown-up in your congregation grousing that "young people should come to church more these days," you've got some stats on *your* side![2]

Overall, the percentage of Americans who seldom or never attend church services is going up.[3] Why? I suspect the key reason is this: people will do what they decide is worth doing. They'll commit time and energy to activities and causes that they believe are important and that benefit them in some way.

If a church finds its pews mostly empty on Sunday mornings, what's the most logical conclusion? That something's wrong with the people who are staying away? That doesn't sound right to me.

The early church didn't spend time worrying about whether people "went to church." They were too busy *being* the church.

In the Acts of the Apostles, Luke reports that the earliest believers met together *every day*. They prayed, they heard the apostles teach, they shared meals—they shared more than that, actually. They sold whatever they owned and used the money to take care of one another's needs. They didn't have a strategy for "growing the church." Instead, they loved one another and loved their neighbors, and God "added daily to the community those who were being saved" (verse 47; see Acts 2:42-47).

Was Luke, who was writing several decades later, looking at the early church with the rose-colored glasses of nostalgia? Maybe. But other sources, too, tell us that what most attracted people to the early church wasn't what they believed but how they lived. Tertullian, an early third-century North African priest, wrote that "it is mainly the deeds of a love so noble that lead many [nonbelievers] to put a brand upon us. See, they say, how they love one another."[4]

The lessons seem pretty clear: What draws people to church, on Sunday mornings or at any other time, is its *mission*. People want to know they are loved, and want a community where they can show love in return. When the church is asking, not "How do we get more people here?" but "How do we love people wherever they are?" then it's living up to its calling. Then it really is acting as what the Apostles' Creed calls "the holy catholic church."

The Holy Catholic Church

In the New Testament, the original Greek word for "church" is *ekklesia* (source of the English word *ecclesiastical*, which means, more or less, "churchy"). *Ekklesia* means "called out." An old song for kids gets it right: the church is not a building or a steeple, "the church is a people."[5] The church is not simply random individuals who choose to get together. It is a nonbiological family, a tribe that is open to anyone and everyone, who God has "called out" of the world. As Jesus said, his church doesn't belong to this world (John 17:14).

But Jesus' church isn't "called out" of the world in order to leave it behind! Maybe we can think about the church as being "called forward," like someone being picked out of a crowd to perform a special task. God calls the church forward to a different kind of life: the life of holiness.

Being *holy* is not synonymous with being perfect! No reasonable person could look at the church today and conclude that it is perfect. And being holy isn't the same thing as being "holier than thou"—looking down our noses at people outside of the church, pretending we are better than they are. "Holy" simply means different, unique, "other." God has chosen the church to perform a unique service: to embody God's love for the world. When the church is carrying out that single mission, it is holy.

The church can and does fulfill its mission in many different ways, and through many different traditions. Those differences sometimes make it hard to see that God's holy church is also *catholic*—universal in scope, including people from all backgrounds and countries, cultures, and languages. The church reaches all around the world. There is not institutional unity among all Christians, but there is spiritual unity. Jesus did pray that all his followers would be one (John 17:21), and Christians can do more to make that unity more visible in the world, but Christian unity doesn't ultimately depend on what we do. Like our salvation, our unity is a gift from God. It's a done deal. Whether or not we ever would have chosen one another, we're all sisters and brothers because God, in Christ, has chosen us!

By talking about "the holy catholic church," the Apostles' Creed puts our individual experiences as church members into bigger perspective. You are more than a person in the pews at a local church building. You are a part of God's epic plan to love the world! That's a pretty amazing identity.

The Communion of Saints

That identity is the best reason I know, in the end, *not* to want too many "skip Sundays." No, the church isn't perfect. Yes, we can always do a better job of loving people. But nowhere else can you hear that you belong to this subversive social movement God has unleashed on the unsuspecting world. Nowhere else will you learn that God has chosen you to be an agent of light and life and love that gives people hope not only for a life to come but also for this life.

Nowhere else, in other words, will you learn that you're on God's "team." You are one of the saints.

It's true! "Saints" aren't just people who've been given that title in front of their name. When the Apostle Paul wrote letters, he addressed them "to the saints" in various cities—Corinth, Rome, Ephesus, Colossae, Philippi—meaning all who were "dearly loved by God" (Romans 1:7). And the roster of this saintly team includes names not only from all around the world but also throughout all of time.

The Apostles' Creed reference to "the communion of saints" isn't so much a reference to the Lord's Supper—although when we share the bread and cup in worship, one thing we're doing is making a symbolic statement of our connection to one another—as it is a statement that *all* whom God has chosen for the mission of loving the world, no matter where or when they lived, are connected to one another.

Hebrews 11 is one of the Bible's most memorable affirmations of this reality. The author of Hebrews reminds me of a tour guide leading us, as though we were a group of sightseers, through a portrait gallery. Look, there's

Noah! There's Abraham and Sarah! There's Moses! And there are many more, some of whom are mentioned only in passing, some of whose names are no longer known. But they were all people whom God chose to play a part in the divine mission, and they all trusted that God would keep God's promises to them.

Then, as the tour is about to come to an end, our guide points us to the most important portrait of all: "Jesus, faith's pioneer and perfecter" (Hebrews 12:2). Because of him, we are forever joined to those who have gone before us. They are now "a great cloud of witnesses surrounding us" (12:1), cheering us on as we follow the trail Jesus blazed, as they did.

God's Future Is Now

So if being the church matters more than going to church—if following Jesus by loving others is what the church is all about—how concerned should we be about how many people do or don't come? After all, can't we love God anywhere? Aren't there neighbors we can serve all around us, every day?

Of course—but the church, gathered together for worship and service, is a visible sign that God's future is on the way. God has planned "to bring all things together in Christ" (Ephesians 1:10). In the church, imperfect and limited though it is, that plan is taking shape before our eyes, and before the world's.

Some Questions to Think About

- How often do you go to church? Why?
- Based on his description of the early church in Acts 2, how would Luke react if he visited your church?
- What are some specific, practical ways your congregation carries out the church's mission of loving one another and loving its neighbors?
- How much does your congregation reflect the diversity of the catholic, or universal, church?
- Which "saints" from the past—the church's past, or your personal past—are you most glad to be connected to, and why?

REFLECT WITH SCRIPTURE

Read 1 Corinthians 12:12-27. These verses are part of the Apostle Paul's extended description of the church as "the body of Christ."

- Why does Paul say Christ is like a body?
- What part of Christ's body do you think you are most like, and why? Would others in the church say the same about you?
- When have you heard about, or seen for yourself, different parts of Christ's body trying to "go it alone," or claiming they didn't need the other parts? What happened?
- How have you experienced the different parts of Christ's body suffering or celebrating together?
- What images or metaphors for the church do you think Paul might use if he were writing today?

SUGGESTED ACTIVITIES

Learn Your Church's History

Interview one or more people in your congregation who know about its history. Ask questions such as: Who founded our church? Why did they start this congregation when and where they did? What are some of our church's biggest accomplishments? What about some of its biggest challenges? How would our community be different today if our church wasn't here? What hopes do you have for this congregation's future? If possible (and with your interviewees' permission), record your conversations for others in the congregation to see and hear, both now and in the future.

Puzzle Piece Relay Race

In a group setting, form two teams of players. Get two identical, inexpensive, *small* jigsaw puzzles (fifty pieces or fewer; check with local dollar stores) and place them on two tables, all pieces facedown and shuffled. Have players run to a table, one at a time, and turn over pieces until they can connect two of them. Players connect the pieces, turn the others back over, and run back to tag the next player. The team that finishes assembling its puzzle first wins. After the race, talk about how completing this task is like and unlike the church fulfilling its mission. (Adapted from The Asset Edge, "Puzzle Relay—An Inspiring Way to End a Meeting," August 17, 2010, http://theassetedge.net/blog/?p=597.)

Visit Another Church

Arrange to visit another Christian congregation for their main worship service one weekend. If possible, go to a congregation unlike your own in significant ways (style of worship, ethnic makeup, etc.). What differences between your congregation and this one do you find the most interesting, and why? What do you think your congregation might learn from the one you visit? What evidence of the two congregations' shared Christian faith do you see?

WHAT DO YOU BELIEVE?

A new thought I had about the church in this session:

_____

A question I still have about the church after this session:

_____

One thing I want others to know I believe about the church:

_____

5.

THE FORGIVENESS OF SINS

I believe in…
  the forgiveness of sins…

PRAY A PSALM

The LORD is compassionate and merciful,
    very patient, and full of faithful love.
God won't always play the judge;
    he won't be angry forever.
He doesn't deal with us according to our sin
      or repay us according to our wrongdoing,
      because as high as heaven is above the earth,
      that's how large God's faithful love is for those who honor him.
As far as east is from west—
      that's how far God has removed our sin from us.

                                        —Psalm 103:8-12

GET THE CONVERSATION ROLLING

Roll a six-sided die and answer the corresponding question from the list below.

1. What's your earliest memory of getting caught doing something you knew was wrong?
2. Has someone ever taken the blame for something you've done? What happened?
3. Have you ever taken the blame for something someone else has done? Why?
4. What's your opinion of the old saying "Forgive and forget"? Explain.
5. What's your opinion of the old saying "The devil made me do it"?
6. Are some actions unforgivable? Why or why not?

CONSIDER THE CREED

A Vote for Forgiveness

In eighth grade, I agreed to be my friend Greg's "campaign manager" when he ran for student body president. Truthfully, there wasn't much campaigning to manage. Election season at the school lasted all of one week—just enough time for each candidate to make one statement to the student body during morning announcements, to hang a poster or two in the halls, and to hand out flyers. The race was nothing more than a popularity contest.

Unfortunately for Greg, his only opponent was a very popular cheerleader. (I know, it sounds like an episode of a bad Disney Channel sitcom.) It became clear, very early on, that Greg had no chance. Sure enough, he received only a handful of votes on election day.

Years later, I'm still ashamed to admit none of those votes was mine. When push came to shove, I went with the crowd and voted against my own candidate, and my friend.

That was bad enough. But even worse, when Greg later lamented his skimpy share of the electorate, I let slip what I'd done.

"What?!?!" He was understandably upset. "You were supposed to be my campaign manager!"

"Well," I said, knowing I'd done a really rotten thing but wanting to justify it somehow, "everyone knew she would win anyway!"

I'm amazed Greg didn't punch me in the face.

But not only did he refrain from giving me the swift kick I thoroughly deserved, he remained my friend. I'm not sure I would have, had I been him. I'd betrayed him. I'd let him down. I'd actively chosen against him, then tried to defend it. And I'm not even sure I ever told him I was sorry.

But Greg forgave me. Our friendship continued.

We human beings too often treat (well, more accurately, mistreat) our relationship with God the same way I treated my relationship with Greg. We take God for granted, and we actively choose against God. We betray God; we let God down. Sometimes we even try to justify it. Sometimes we don't even say we're sorry. The Apostle Paul puts the situation this way: "All have sinned and fall short of God's glory" (Romans 3:23).

But in his very next breath, Paul says "all are treated as righteous freely by [God's] grace because of a ransom that was paid by Christ Jesus" (Romans 3:24). God is merciful. Not content to let us destroy our most important relationship, God forgives us. God treats us with completely undeserved and unconditional kindness by giving us Jesus Christ.

The Apostles' Creed declares the early church's belief in the forgiveness of sins. Christians have always believed that Jesus died and was raised in order to save us from the spiritual consequences of our sins. "The wages that sin pays are death," Paul wrote elsewhere, "but God's gift is eternal life in Christ Jesus our Lord" (Romans 6:23).

Jesus Christ is God's vote for forgiveness!

At One Through Atonement

The Creed talks about "sins," the individual wrongs that we commit. Yet our particular sins are only part of the problem.

If solving the problem of sins were as easy as obeying instruction from on high, humanity would be better off and the world would be a better place. But, as Paul recognized, we can't simply make the choice to stop sinning, no matter how much we want to (see Romans 7:15-21). We commit sins because *the power of sin* has sunk its claws into our species.

Sin is an actively hostile power, intent on opposing God's good will, determined to do all it can to rip us out of relationship with God. This idea wasn't Paul's invention. We find it, for example, in the story of the very first murder. Before Cain killed his brother Abel, God warned Cain that "sin will be waiting at the door ready to strike! It will entice you, but you must rule over it" (Genesis 4:7). Cain couldn't, of course—and neither has any human being since.

It's not necessary that human beings sin; it's not a part of who we were created to be. It just turns out to be inevitable. The only human being who has never succumbed to sin is Jesus Christ (Hebrews 4:15). When we say we believe Jesus is fully human, that's the reason why. Since Jesus alone stayed completely faithful to God's will all his days, he's more fully human than any of us!

In Christian theology, Jesus' work of saving us from sin is called the atonement. Jesus atones for what we have done wrong—he "makes up for it." He makes our relationship with God possible when we, left to ourselves, would throw it away.

But *how*, exactly? There's never been universal agreement. The New Testament offers multiple images of how Jesus' death and resurrection bring forgiveness. Over the centuries, theologians have identified three main "models," or ways of understanding, the atonement.

Substitutionary Atonement

According to this model, Jesus died in our place. Sometimes this model speaks of Jesus paying a penalty for our sin, or even a ransom in order to bring us back to God (as in Paul's words from Romans, quoted above). Other times, it pictures Jesus as a sacrifice offered up to God, the same way the ancient Israelites offered sacrifices to please God. In either case, Jesus is taking upon himself the consequences of sin that we rightly deserve. Because Jesus does, God regards us as innocent: "Christ himself suffered on account of sins, once for all, the righteous one on behalf of the unrighteous. He did this in order to bring you into the presence of God" (1 Peter 3:18).

Many early Christians found support for their belief about Jesus as our substitute in Isaiah's prophecy about a suffering servant: "He was pierced because of our rebellions and crushed because of our crimes. He bore the punishment that made us whole; by his wounds we are healed" (Isaiah 53:5). Certainly, the model of substitutionary atonement has been the most influential in the history of Western Christianity. It takes God's law and justice seriously, and stresses how serious sin is: nothing short of the death of God's own Son can make up for it.

But this model also raises some difficult questions. Is justice really served if God allows or causes an innocent victim to suffer so the guilty can go free? And does Jesus dying in our place really take away our sin, or is his death some kind of "scheme" that merely pretends it no longer matters?

Moral Influence

According to this model, Jesus' willingness to die for us is the ultimate demonstration of God's love. When we see the extent of God's love, we are moved to repent of our sins and begin living with love for God and our neighbor. Jesus tells his disciples, "This is my commandment: love each other just as I have loved you. No one has greater love than to give up one's life for one's friends" (John 15:12-13).

This model mirrors one of the most famous of Bible verses: "God so loved the world that he gave his only Son" (John 3:16). It also highlights the importance of our response to God's forgiveness. If we do not grow in our ability to extend pardon to those who have wronged us, then have we really received God's pardon? "As the Lord forgave you," the author of Colossians urges, "so also forgive each other" (3:13).

But the moral influence model leaves some hard questions of its own unanswered. What if someone is *not* emotionally moved by Jesus' death—does the lack of response make it all for nothing? And does Jesus' death actually, objectively change anything about our relationship with God, regardless of what we feel (or don't) about it?

Christus Victor

According to the *Christus Victor* model (Latin for "Christ the conqueror"), Jesus deals with sin as a divine warrior. His death and resurrection are his triumph over the power of sin, as well as the powers of evil and death itself: "God's Son appeared for this purpose: to destroy the works of the devil" (1 John 3:8).

This model sees forgiveness of sin as one aspect of a much larger conflict between God and Satan. It does *not* view the battle as a contest of equals; God's victory over evil is always certain. But we struggle with sin because we're caught in the crossfire. The devil attempts to trick and trap us, making us serve evil instead of God (2 Timothy 2:26). But Jesus' death, this model says, turned out to be God's tricking and trapping of Satan! Jesus "destroy[ed] the one who holds the power over death—the devil—by dying" (Hebrews 2:14).

The *Christus Victor* model may shed some light on one of the more confusing lines in the Apostles' Creed. After saying they believe Jesus "was crucified, died, and was buried," some churches add, "He descended into hell." The line can also be translated "descended to the dead," and that's accurate, because the Creed is, on one level, simply stressing in one more way that Jesus *really* died. But the other translation could suggest that, between his death and resurrection, Jesus actually did go to hell—not as a punishment for sin (since he lived a sinless life), but in order to take God's fight right to the devil!

Search on "Harrowing of Hell," and you'll see there's a long tradition of Christian art that shows Jesus freeing people from the realm of the dead in between his crucifixion and resurrection. No Bible verse spells out that Jesus did this, but there is one intriguing mention of him going "by the Spirit . . . to preach to the spirits in prison" (1 Peter 3:19). Did Jesus stage a rescue mission to hell on Holy Saturday? We don't know for certain, but the idea would be right at home in the *Christus Victor* model.

This model takes seriously the truth that human beings have become captives to a power we cannot control or defeat, but that God can—and does. Jesus' death really, objectively conquers sin. But this model, too, raises questions. Perhaps the most pressing one: if Jesus has definitively defeated the power of sin for everyone, why is it important for anyone to make a personal response to what Jesus has done?

Forgive as We Have Been Forgiven

None of these three models of the atonement, by itself, says everything Christians want and need to say about the forgiveness of sins. When we look at them together, they can help us appreciate just how important the forgiveness of sins is.

But none of the models matters much if we don't also believe that because God has forgiven our sins in Jesus, we are called to forgive sins too. Jesus wanted to make sure his disciples understood that God's forgiveness of humans had to translate into humans' forgiveness of each other. "If you forgive others their sins," he taught, "your heavenly Father will also forgive you. But if you don't forgive others, neither will your Father forgive your sins" (Matthew 6:14-15).

God doesn't forgive our sins so we can keep on sinning! God forgives us to free us from crippling fear and burdensome guilt, and so we will be free to extend forgiveness and love to our neighbors. If God's forgiving us our sins doesn't lead to us forgiving those who sin against us, then we haven't really experienced God's pardon, and we are still enslaved to the power of sin.

Jesus' teaching about the connection between God's forgiveness of us and our forgiveness of others sounds difficult. It doesn't seem to square with what the church, following Scripture, says about being saved by grace alone, through faith alone (Ephesians 2:8-10). But maybe Jesus means something like this: There is nothing we can do to save ourselves, it's true...but there's plenty we can do, sadly, to keep God's salvation from changing us into the kind of people God wants us to be right now. There's plenty we can do to "suppress the Spirit," if we choose, as powerful as the Spirit is (1 Thessalonians 5:19), and refusing to forgive others is one of them.

Forgiveness doesn't mean pretending other people have done nothing wrong, or that we are not hurt by their actions. And it doesn't mean putting ourselves in a situation where we are almost certain to be hurt again. But it does mean refusing to let the way they wronged us define us, or them. It means refusing to nurse grudges or seek revenge; it means denying the past any power to control us. When we forgive other people's sins against us, we move forward into a better future that God has in store.

Some Questions to Think About

- When have you been most aware of God's forgiveness of your sins?
- Which of the three traditional models of the atonement do you find most helpful, and why?
- When have you had a hard time forgiving someone? What did you do (or what are you now doing) about it?
- Since we believe God has forgiven us in Jesus, do we still need to pray for forgiveness? Why or why not?

REFLECT WITH SCRIPTURE

Read Luke 7:36-50.

- Why is Simon, the Pharisee, so scandalized by the woman who interrupts his dinner with Jesus, and by Jesus' reaction to her?
- How does the story that Jesus tells Simon about the two debtors apply to the woman? How does it apply to Simon?
- How do you show gratitude to God for forgiving your sins in Jesus?
- How would you respond to someone who said, "I don't have any sins God needs to forgive"?
- How would you respond to someone who said, "God could never forgive *my* sins"?
- How does Jesus' forgiveness of the woman's sins show who he is?

SUGGESTED ACTIVITIES

Stories of Forgiveness

Either search the Internet or look through recent issues of newspapers and magazines for true stories of forgiveness. (Be sure you are using a reputable, trustworthy source.) Prepare a brief report on the story that you can share with your youth group. Be sure to identify who was involved, what happened that was forgiven, and what were the direct results, if any, of the wronged person's choice to forgive. Also, choose a Bible verse you think applies to the story that you found, and be ready to explain why.

Act a Parable of Forgiveness

Read Matthew 18:21-35 and/or Luke 15:11-32. What do each of these stories teach about forgiveness? With a group of friends, plan and act out a skit that "translates" the parable(s) into a modern setting. Record your performance to show others in your congregation.

Film and Faith

In *Spider-Man 3* (2007), Peter Parker, aka Spider-Man, faces off against the Sandman, a criminal changed into a shape-shifting sand form by a freak accident. (Hate when that happens!) Sandman killed Peter's uncle years before, and Peter spends much of the film seeking revenge. Watch Spidey and Sandman's final confrontation (2:06:10–2:09:26).

- Is Peter right to tell Sandman, "We always have a choice"? Why or why not?
- Why is Peter able to forgive Sandman?
- What does this scene suggest about the power of forgiveness?

WHAT DO YOU BELIEVE?

A new thought I had about forgiveness in this session:

_____

A question I still have about forgiveness after this session:

_____

One thing I want others to know I believe about forgiveness:

_____

6.

THE RESURRECTION
OF THE BODY

I believe in…
     the resurrection of the body and the life everlasting.

PRAY A PSALM

I always put the LORD in front of me;
     I will not stumble because he is on my right side.
That's why my heart celebrates and my mood is joyous;
     yes, my whole body will rest in safety
     because you won't abandon my life to the grave;
     you won't let your faithful follower see the pit.
You teach me the way of life.
     In your presence is total celebration.
Beautiful things are always in your right hand.

     —Psalm 16:8-11

GET THE CONVERSATION ROLLING

Roll a six-sided die and answer the corresponding question from the list below.

1. Are you basically an optimist or a pessimist? Why?
2. What's your favorite depiction of the future from TV, books, or the movies? Why?
3. What about the twenty-first century makes you the most hopeful?
4. What about the twenty-first century worries you the most?
5. What image first comes to mind when you think about heaven?
6. What about your personal future are you most looking forward to?

CONSIDER THE CREED

Hope for the Future?

Are you looking forward to the future?

On the one hand, the early twenty-first century is an amazing time. From the World Wide Web and smartphones to 3-D printing and advanced robotics, humanity seems to be making great progress.

On the other hand, we're also living in a time of great uncertainty. The global threat of terrorism, the ever-growing inequality gap between society's wealthiest members and everyone else, the present dangers posed by climate change....you know the dangers and challenges facing the world.

Every age, of course, has known both promise and peril when looking ahead. And, for the last two thousand years, the Christian church has dared to face the future, not with optimism—because, let's face it, sometimes we human beings don't inspire much optimism—but with *hope*. Because we believe God raised Jesus from the dead, we believe that our future, and the future of the whole creation, is safe and secure in God's good and powerful hands.

The Apostles' Creed concludes with two very specific affirmations about the future: "I believe in . . . the resurrection of the body and the life everlasting."

The Resurrection of the Body

If you're a fan of horror movies, the phrase "resurrection of the body" may conjure up images of Dr. Frankenstein shocking a cobbled-together cadaver with electricity in his lab, triumphantly shouting, "It's alive! It's *alive!*"—or maybe the zombies of *The Walking Dead* shambling down the deserted, postapocalyptic highways of Atlanta.

The Creed isn't talking about some nightmare scenario. The resurrection of the body refers to the Christian hope that God will give us new life after we die.

My grandmother was a devout Christian. Anytime my sister and I spent the night at her house, she'd make sure we said our bedtime prayers. She taught us an old prayer you may have heard too: "Now I lay me down to sleep; I pray the Lord my soul to keep. Should I die before I wake, I pray the Lord my soul to take."

She loved us and meant well. But the Christian hope of life after death *isn't* about having an immortal soul. *We don't.* Scripture consistently teaches, not that we "have" souls, but that we are *embodied souls.* God infused us with the breath of life, God's own breath (remember—God's creative, life-giving Spirit) when fashioning us from the dust (Genesis 2:7). Human beings are integrated, inseparable body *and* soul, flesh *and* spirit.

And when we die—*we die.* No ifs, ands, or buts. Like the Wicked Witch of the West, we are not "merely dead," we are "really, most sincerely dead!" We are mortal—body and soul, flesh and spirit. Nothing about us "naturally" continues on after death. God "alone has immortality" (1 Timothy 6:16). Like Jesus, when we die, we are dead and buried; we descend to the dead. There's just no getting around it: we are dust, and to dust we return (see Genesis 3:19).

The resurrection of the body will be, literally, an honest-to-God miracle! We know this because Jesus himself is "the first crop of the harvest of those who have died" (1 Corinthians 15:20). *He* was really and truly dead, but now he is really and truly "alive forever and always" (Revelation 1:18). And because he lives, we will live too (John 14:19). But our immortal lives will be no less a free gift from God than our mortal ones were.

In the new life God alone gives, we will still be ourselves. In fact, we will be more ourselves than we ever can be in this life, because we will no longer have to struggle against sin and evil. But we won't be like a river returning to the ocean, all sense of what makes us unique washed away. We will be our individual, identifiable selves—not vague spirits floating around like mists in heaven. That's why we profess belief in the resurrection of the body.

Granted, we're pushing language to its limits as we try to describe what our future existence will be like. But we're in good company. The Apostle Paul knew that "flesh and blood can't inherit God's kingdom" (1 Corinthians 15:50). Just the same, he said our physical bodies would be raised as spiritual bodies (15:44-49).

To believe in the resurrection of the body is to believe that our lives here and now matter to God, just as they matter to us and to those who know us. While we are all equal before God, we are not interchangeable, mix-and-match widgets. God will save and make perfect everything that makes you *you* in the life to come.

The Life Everlasting

I mentioned *Star Wars* back in our second session, but my most enduring sci-fi passion has been *Star Trek*. Something about the voyages of the starship *Enterprise* as its crew seeks out strange new worlds fills me with a sense of wonder like little else.

I felt it again when watching (as of this writing) the most recent Star Trek movie, *Star Trek Beyond*. Early in the film, the *Enterprise* visits Starbase Yorktown: a gigantic, glittering city in space, full of impossibly elegant architecture and residents who have come from all corners of the galaxy. It's a beautiful place, and it represents the astonishing things we humans can achieve when we put our minds to it.

Christian faith's vision of the future includes a gigantic, glittering city too—but it's not one we build. In Revelation, the Bible's last book, the first-century Christian prophet John sees "the holy city, New Jerusalem, coming down out of heaven from God" (21:2). Like Starbase Yorktown, New Jerusalem boasts incredible architecture (it's a perfect square, John says, of glass and gold, with jewel-studded foundations) and inhabitants who hail from everywhere—

"a great crowd that no one could number...from every nation, tribe, people and language" (7:9). But humanity is not the center of this city. In New Jerusalem, God is in the middle of it all—"the Lord God Almighty and the Lamb," Jesus Christ (21:22).

New Jerusalem represents God's re-creation of all things, a new heaven and a new earth where God and humanity live together again as they did in the garden of Eden. But God's promised future is not a return to the garden! As American theologian Shirley Guthrie wrote:

> "The Bible chooses...the picture of city life to talk about what eternal life will be like. A city is a place where there is work to be done, where there is excitement and action....[Heaven] will be a place in which there will always be new things to learn, new things to do, new tasks to perform in service of the living God."[1]

"The life everlasting" includes our personal futures, but it's also so much bigger! We Christians look forward not just to our own salvation, but to the time when God will be "making all things new" (Revelation 21:5).

On God's Holy Mountain

Ancient Israel's faith did not include the expectation of personal resurrection until sometime during the Babylonian exile, some six centuries before Jesus. Even so, much of the Old Testament's imagery of God's promised future continues to shape Christian hope.

For example, look at the description of life in days to come that the prophet Isaiah shares. He says that Mount Zion, "the mountain of the LORD's house" (2:2), will be the center of not only Judah's life but also that of all the nations. Imagine: throngs of men, women, and children from around the globe, faces of every color turned toward Jerusalem, excitedly urging one another, in all the world's languages, "Come, let's go up to the LORD's mountain" (2:3). The God of Israel will still be met on Mount Zion, but not by Israelites alone.

Isaiah preached in a time, like ours, that was troubled by international conflict. That context makes his vision all the more breathtaking. He makes the amazing announcement that all nations will pour into Jerusalem eager for God's *torah*, God's guidance, in the ways of peace. As the old spiritual sings, the nations will lay down their sword and shield and study war no more. They will transform tools of death into tools of life. Now wielding plowshares and pruning hooks, the nations will know (to borrow language from Ecclesiastes 3) a time for planting and for healing and for peace.

How did Isaiah's war-weary, frightened first audience react to this daring dream? Some, perhaps, had trouble believing that the nations could ever experience such harmony. Others reacted with hostility at the suggestion that Israel's God would extend *torah* to enemies and outsiders. Still others might have greeted Isaiah's words as a beautiful wish for the future, but irrelevant to the difficult realities of the present.

Isaiah leaves no doubt: his vision of the future—more accurately, *God's* vision, communicated through him—*does* matter now. "O house of Jacob," he calls, "come, let us walk in the light of the LORD!" (2:5 NRSV). He appeals for them to take real steps toward living as though that day had already arrived.

Did they take those steps? I'm sure some did and others didn't.

The more pressing question is, will *we*? What practical difference does belief in the life everlasting make *today*?

An Example From Ephrata

I live not far from Ephrata, Pennsylvania, where the cloisters of a remarkable eighteenth-century community of German Protestant mystics have been lovingly preserved and restored. The "Brothers" and "Sisters" of Ephrata lived like monks. Every midnight, they roused from their hard, narrow beds (little more than wooden planks) to gather for a three-hour service of hymns and prayers. They believed Jesus would return some midnight and wanted to be found awake when he did.

When I tour the Ephrata Cloisters, I'm tempted to dismiss the Brothers' and Sisters' ascetic excess as well intentioned but misguided. But isn't it possible these unusual mystics have a lesson to teach us? They knew something was wrong with this world—they knew this world desperately needs God's renewal—and they refused to be conformed to it (see Romans 12:2).

Their focus on the new world to come led them to "live honorably" in the midst of the old. Their piety embraced work that benefited not only themselves but also their neighbors. In the Revolutionary War, the Brothers and Sisters cared for some five hundred of General Washington's wounded soldiers after the nearby Battle of Brandywine. They tenderly nursed many men back to health, but at the cost of infection and disease that, ultimately, hastened the religious community's demise. One soldier who survived later wrote, "Until I entered the walls of Ephrata, I had no idea of pure and practical Christianity. Not that I was ignorant of the forms, or even the doctrines of religion. I knew it in theory before; I saw it in practice then."[2]

When we really believe in the life everlasting, we can't rest content and complacent with this life, this world, as it is. "Life," says one twentieth-century statement of Christian faith, "is a gift to be received with gratitude and a task to be pursued with courage."[3] Yes, humanity is sinful, living in a fallen world; and, no, "the present form of this world" will not last forever (1 Corinthians 7:31 NRSV). The Apostles' Creed doesn't answer all our questions about God's promised future, but it tells us all we need to know: it *is* God's, and it will be good!

Until it arrives, this world is still God's world, and we still live in it as God's chosen and commissioned people. Remember the definition we're given of everlasting life in John's Gospel: "This is eternal life: to know you, the only true God, and Jesus Christ whom you sent" (John 17:3). Heaven is not so much a place as it is a person: Jesus Christ, God's only Son, our Lord, with whom we can live starting today. We have this message of everlasting life to share, in word and in deed—and the Apostles' Creed helps us share it.

Some Questions to Think About

- What will be the best thing about the life everlasting?
- How do you react to the idea that we don't "have souls" but are "embodied souls"?
- How does the hope of life everlasting motivate you to act in this life?
- How do you react to the statement "Heaven is not so much a place as it is a person"?

REFLECT WITH SCRIPTURE

Read Revelation 21:1-5 and 21:22–22:6. The early Christian prophet John received a vision of the New Jerusalem—the new world God promises to create at the end of time.

- What will change because "God's dwelling is…with humankind" (verse 3) in the world to come?
- What features of John's vision appeal to you the most? Which ones, if any, confuse you?
- Why is there no temple (the special meeting place of God and humanity) in the New Jerusalem (21:22)?
- How do the trees' leaves "for the healing of the nations" (22:2) indicate that God's promised future is about more than personal salvation?
- What modern images would you use to describe everlasting life and God's new world?

SUGGESTED ACTIVITIES

News From the New Jerusalem

Recall Shirley Guthrie's statement that in the heavenly city, "there will always be new things to learn, new things to do, new tasks to perform in service of the living God." What do you think one of those new things and tasks might be? Imagine you are writing a news story about something that has happened in the New Jerusalem. What would your headline be? Draw a website page or the front page of a newspaper featuring your headline and lead paragraph. Be sure to draw a picture to go with your story.

Ask About Heaven

Ask people you know what they think heaven will be like. Don't judge their answers; instead, once you have gathered several responses, look for what people's responses have in common. Try to ask people of different ages, ethnicities, and beliefs. As you review your findings, ask yourself:

- What common hopes do people seem to have about heaven?
- Does Scripture reinforce or question these hopes, and how?

If possible, get people's permission to record their responses. Prepare a multimedia presentation to share with your youth group and congregation.

Film and Faith

Watch the scene from *Tomorrowland* (2015) in which Casey sees the incredibly advanced world of the future (0:31:15–0:36:17).

- How is the future world that Casey sees like and unlike the future world John sees in Revelation?
- When Casey's vision ends, she is left longing for the future she saw. How do Christians cope with the gap between the world as it is and the future, God-promised world that John sees?
- *Tomorrowland* is a movie that says dreamers will shape the future. How is this philosophy like and unlike what Christians believe about how the future will be shaped?

WHAT DO YOU BELIEVE?

A new thought I had about God's promised future in this session:

_____

A question I still have about God's promised future after this session:

_____

One thing I want others to know I believe about God's promised future:

_____

NOTES

1. "The Apostles' Creed, Ecumenical Version," *The United Methodist Hymnal* (Nashville: The United Methodist Publishing House), #882.

INTRODUCTION

1. See Presbyterian Church (U.S.A.), *Book of Confessions*, Study Edition (Louisville: Geneva Press, 1999), 16.
2. From a video interview in "This I Believe (The Creed) Song Story," by Hillsong Worship, Hillsong Collected, July 3, 2014, http://hillsong.com/collected /blog/2014/07/this-i-believe-the-creed-song-story/#.V751PaJyxm8, see 2:03–3:09.

CHAPTER 1

1. Brooke James, "World Renowned Scientist Michio Kaku Proves Existence Of God," *Science World Report*, June 13, 2016, http://www.scienceworldreport .com/articles/42042/20160613/world-renowned-scientist-michio -kaku-proves-existence-god.htm.
2. Michio Kaku, "We Physicists Are the Only Scientists Who Can Say the Word 'God' and Not Blush," *The Big Think*, n.d., http://bigthink.com/dr-kakus -universe/we-physicists-are-the-only-scientists-who-can-say-the-word-god -and-not-blush.
3. "Michio Kaku's Opinion on God," interview by Dr. Kiki, uploaded August 20, 2011, www.youtube.com/watch?v=SBB2qHgZvLY.
4. Ibid., see 01:05–01:53.

5. See Alon Goshen-Gottstein, "God the Father in Rabbinic Judaism and Christianity: Transformed Background or Common Ground?" *Journal of Ecumenical Studies* 38, no. 4 (Spring 2001), http://www.jcrelations.net /od+the+Father+in+Rabbinic+Judaism+and+Christianity%3A +Transformed+Background+or+Common+Ground%3F.2771.0.html?L=3.
6. The Revised Common Lectionary, Year C, Proper 19 (24th Sunday in Ordinary Time; 17th Sunday after Pentecost), http://lectionary.library.vanderbilt.edu /texts.php?id=279.

CHAPTER 2

1. J. R. R. Tolkien, "On Fairy-Stories," in *Essays Presented to Charles Williams*, ed. C. S. Lewis (London: Oxford University Press, 1947), quoted in Sarah Arthur, *The God-Hungry Imagination* (Nashville: Upper Room Books, 2007), 86, http://bit.ly/2aqQ4Jd.
2. William H. Parker, "Tell Me the Stories of Jesus," 1885, http://www.hymnary .org/text/tell_me_the_stories_of_jesus_i_love_to.
3. See Melanie B. Smith, "Jesuses in Alabama," *The Decatur Daily*, December 24, 2006, http://archive.decaturdaily.com/decaturdaily/news/061224/jesuses.shtml.
4. Brian Palmer, "Happy Birthday, Dear Yeshua, Happy Birthday to You!" *Slate*, December 24, 2008, http://www.slate.com/articles/news_and_politics /explainer/2008/12/happy_birthday_dear_yeshua_happy_birthday_to_you .html.
5. Behind the Name, "Joshua," n.d., http://www.behindthename.com/name /joshua.
6. Harvey Araton, "Job 1: Putting the Knicks Before the Coach," *The New York Times*, April 11, 2016, http://www.nytimes.com/2016/04/12/sports/basketball /on-the-selection-of-the-knicks-new-coach-a-few-musings-from-a-past -official.html.
7. http://howmanyofme.com/search/.

CHAPTER 3

1. Caffeine Informer, "Red Bull," n.d., http://www.caffeineinformer.com /caffeine-content/red-bull.
2. Mayo Clinic Staff, "Caffeine Content for Coffee, Tea, Soda and More," Mayo Clinic, May 13, 2014, http://www.mayoclinic.org/healthy-lifestyle /nutrition-and-healthy-eating/in-depth/caffeine/art-20049372?pg=2.
3. Center for Science in the Public Interest, "Caffeine Chart," n.d., https://cspinet .org/eating-healthy/ingredients-of-concern/caffeine-chart.

4. See Center for Science in the Public Interest, "Beware of These Effects of Caffeine on the Body," August 24, 2015, https://cspinet.org/tip /beware-these-effects-caffeine-body.
5. PR Newswire, "Global Energy Drinks Market 2015–2021: Insights, Market Size, Share, Growth, Trends Analysis and Forecasts for the $61 Billion Industry," September 3, 2015, http://www.prnewswire.com/news-releases /global-energy-drinks-market-2015-2021-insights-market-size-share-growth -trends-analysis-and-forecasts-for-the-61-billion-industry-300137637.html.
6. Elsevier, "Dangers of Adolescent Energy Drink Consumption for the Heart: Cardiologists Urge Physicians, Parents, Educators to Monitor Adolescents' Energy Drink Consumption More Closely," April 1, 2015, https://www.elsevier .com/about/press-releases/research-and-journals/dangers-of -adolescent-energy-drink-consumption-for-the-heart-cardiologists-urge -physicians,-parents,-educators-to-monitor-adolescents-energy-drink -consumption-more-closely.
7. Karl Barth, *The Faith of the Church* (1958; repr. Eugene, Ore.: Wipf & Stock, 2006), 123-24.

CHAPTER 4

1. Corey Seemiller and Meghan Grace, *Generation Z Goes to College* (San Francisco: Jossey-Bass, 2016), 43.
2. Ibid.
3. Michael Lipka, "What Surveys Say About Worship Attendance—and Why Some Stay Home," Pew Research FactTank, September 13, 2013, http://www .pewresearch.org/fact-tank/2013/09/13/what-surveys-say-about-worship -attendance-and-why-some-stay-home/.
4. Tertullian, Apology, Chapter XXXIX, http://www.ccel.org/ccel/schaff/anf03 .iv.iii.xxxix.html.
5. Richard K. Avery and Donald S. Marsh, "We Are the Church," *The United Methodist Hymnal* (Nashville: The United Methodist Publishing House, 1989), #558.

CHAPTER 6

1. Shirley C. Guthrie, *Christian Doctrine* (Louisville: Westminster John Knox Press, 1994), 390.
2. E. G. Alderfer, *The Ephrata Commune: An Early American Counterculture* (Pittsburgh: University of Pittsburgh Press, 1985), 166, quoted in Doug Ward, "The Ephrata Cloister: A Sabbatarian Commune in Colonial Pennsylvania," n.d., http://www.giveshare.org/churchhistory/ephrata.html#ref1.
3. *The Confession of 1967*, Presbyterian Church (U.S.A.), 9.17, http://www.creeds .net/reformed/conf67.htm.